WHITE TOWERS

WHITE TOWERS

Paul Hirshorn and Steven Izenour

Dear Justin

This is to show you how hard some of the research M.I.T publishes can be!

Don't let big names to ever scare you.

Happy Birth Day

Parviz

The MIT Press

Cambridge, Massachusetts, and London, England

This book was printed and bound
by Halliday Lithograph Corporation
in the United States of America.

**Library of Congress Cataloging
in Publication Data**

Hirshorn, Paul.
  White Towers.

  Includes index.
  I. White Tower (Firm) I. Izenour,
Steven, joint author. II. Title.
TX945.5.W49H57   338.7'61'6479573
79-721   ISBN 0-262-08096-6

Authors' Note

Everyone on the East Coast will recognize these gleaming little white buildings, located in older business districts and along roadside strips, open all night, serving hamburgers and coffee, but few will be aware of their architectural history. The White Tower System was one of the first short-order food chains in the country and a pioneer in a form of food service that has become an integral part of American life. In more than fifty years of development the White Towers have formed a particularly complete and sophisticated set of stylistic variations on one strict symbolic theme—a white building with a tower over its entrance—for one strict functional purpose: selling hamburgers. The appearance of the buildings was always used consciously to project an impression of cleanliness and speedy service with a hint of elegance added to smooth over the modest nature of the establishment. This "image" was maintained over the years by numerable subtle (and some not so subtle) architectural devices that responded to a broad range of constantly changing conditions, such as the use of different materials, the switch from downtown to highway sites, and the need to make both freestanding buildings and applied storefronts appear the same. Over the last fifty years there have been, to be sure, many other examples of chains of commercial buildings produced with flair and style, using evocative materials (often white) and symbolic forms like a tower, but none that we know of have produced such a range of interesting variations on a single theme for so many years. This was directly attributable, in the case of the White Towers, to owners who took a positive delight in tinkering with their buildings, coupled with a staff that had the skill to carry out architectural experiments.

In paying close attention to various White Towers we do not mean to imply that individually they can stand as great works of architecture (although we do admit to our fondness for them and we do have our favorites). Theirs is not a self-conscious Architecture created by a famous architect of the sort that is usually studied and admired, nor is it an unconscious folk vernacular. The White Towers are a series of buildings that set out only to be visible and evocative in order to sell hamburgers, and not to be original or inventive. Their theme is limited architecturally, and the shops have varied little in either size or basic arrangement over five decades. While the location and siting of White Towers has always been handled with insight and sophistication, they have never displayed a sensitivity toward their surroundings, since their purpose has always been served by standing aggressively apart from their neighbors, and their use of bright materials has always guaranteed achieving it. Despite these limitations, the White Towers represent a strong architectural idea. Their strength lies in their numbers, massed as they are on the following pages.

Since White Tower design has been inextricably bound to the growth and development of the White Tower System, we have discussed the company history and goals and how it dealt with changing business conditions. We hope that this case study can shed some light on the nature of commercial architectural design, its conscious use of both signs and symbols, how it incorporates contemporary styles, and the criteria by which it measures its success. In both photographs and text one can see aspects of the growth and development of urban America during the past half-century. In particular it is possible to trace the growth of the fast-food industry along with changes in taste and eating habits, as well as the effects of the shift from a dependence on public transportation to a dependence on private automobiles. The photographs, of course, provide their own amusement by recording fifty years of clothing and automobile styles, signs and prices.

The notion of studying the White Towers in some depth came to us slowly and by chance. Not so much by chance, our interest in White Towers dates from 1970, when we were both working for the architectural firm of Venturi and Rauch in Philadelphia. At the time Denise Scott Brown and Robert Venturi were actively involved in studying the architectural character of the commercial strip and writing *Learning from Las Vegas* (Cambridge, Mass.: MIT Press, 1972, 1977). In the office, roadside awareness was in the air, so when we drove along the commercial strips in and around Philadelphia we began to notice these little white buildings, which had developed enormous visual impact for their size, particularly at night. During the summer of 1970 we sought out and photographed White Towers in the Philadelphia area, and, when we traveled, in Atlantic City, Boston, and Washington. A year later, idle conversation over the counter of a Camden White Tower led to the startling discovery (to us) that the White Tower architect would be visiting that shop on the next day. We hastily arranged for a meeting, gathered together our photographs, and returned on the following afternoon to meet Charles Johnson, who declared his allegiance in his first sentence ("How about a cup of good White Tower coffee, boys?"). An hour of history and recollection followed as Johnson looked at our photographs of his work. Our appetite for White Towers had been stimulated, so we arranged to visit the company headquarters in Stamford, Connecticut, where Johnson showed us the company photographic archives. To us these old photographs, which almost entirely compose the illustrations for this book, were an invaluable resource. They fully documented the development of the White Towers while showing us the rich architectural heritage of the shops that we had photographed. Taken by countless commercial photographers, the photographs varied in quality, but many were strikingly beautiful. Seeing them suggested to us that we escalate our commitment and attempt a serious study of these little buildings.

Aside from its architectural analysis our essay is heavily indebted to interviews with White Tower personnel and to the resources of the company. We would like to thank Brock Saxe, the President of the Tombrock Corporation, of which White Tower now forms one division, for his interest in, and encouragement of, our project, and for placing the resources of the Corporation at our disposal and allowing the reproduction of the photographs in this book. We would also like to thank Vice Presidents Arnold Saxe and Harold Chase, and zone managers Sam Arpaio, Bob Toney, and Eugene Brooks, all of whom have been with White Tower for more than thirty years and whose crystal-clear memories have helped us to document the development of the company. Finally, we owe a large debt of gratitude to Charles Johnson, White Tower's architect for over forty years and the designer of two-thirds of the buildings shown here, for sharing with us his time, his wit, and his experience. The zone managers and Charles Johnson are the sources for the quotations that enliven the text and the captions.

vii

All of the White Towers shown are identified by their company notation, which organizes the buildings chronologically by city. A letter designation (#1A, for example) indicates that the building has been moved or has been built on or near an old location. The photographs have been arranged to show stylistic development, so they fall into a rough chronological order. A geographical index has been provided for those who would like to refer to the White Towers by city.

WHITE TOWERS

In the 1920s urban America was becoming increasingly prosperous and mobile. Working-class families were moving from the industrial centers of cities to the trim, modest houses that were filling in undeveloped suburban land. Working men were no longer walking to their jobs but commuting on an expanding network of electric trolleys, subways, and buses. As their daily travel time increased they began to look for a place to grab an inexpensive bite to eat, on the run, to and from work or across the street from the factory. "Mom and Pop" luncheonettes were around, to be sure, but their food was of uneven quality and people were skeptical about the origin of their hamburger meat, often with reason.

The opportunity was apparent for a chain of strategically placed hamburger stands—obviously clean places selling "wholesome food at a reasonable price with fast service." One of many who saw this opportunity was twenty-three-year-old Thomas E. Saxe of Milwaukee. Saxe was a graduate of the University of Minnesota with a family tradition for business enterprise. His father, J. E. Saxe, who had come from Ireland to Milwaukee in 1900, was a promoter with flair and savvy. At one time or another the elder Saxe ran movie theater chains, taxicab fleets, and sign painting shops, organized dance marathons, and sold real estate as well as running the popular Elgin Lunch in Milwaukee. The younger Saxe began his initial business venture with his father's encouragement, advice, and financial support. By the mid-1920s the White Castle system, which had originated in Wichita, Kansas, in 1921, had expanded its chain to a number of midwestern cities selling five-cent hamburgers in little white buildings. The Saxes had no doubt seen White Castles in Minneapolis during T. E.'s last year at the University there and had decided to start a similar fast-food operation in their hometown of Milwaukee, more than 300 miles to the southeast.

In the fall of 1926 the Saxes found a promising site for the first White Tower on Wisconsin Avenue near the campus of Marquette University. T. E. then went to the S. M. Siesel Construction Company, which had built a number of movie theaters for his father, and described to them the sort of building he wanted. A Siesel draftsman then developed T. E.'s ideas, and the result was Milwaukee #1, which opened for business on November 17, 1926.

I

1. Milwaukee #1 (1926)

2. An early White Tower interior

The exterior of this first design included most of the characteristic elements of all future White Towers—a shining white one-story building with a tower over one corner, above the entrance (Fig. 1). The dominant effect was one of plain, bright, white surfaces. The windows, from residential stock, were small. A modest sign above the windows simply mentioned the name of the new shop. Surface ornament was kept to a minimum. On Milwaukee #1 it was confined to dark green trim along the building's base, roofline, and window sills. The medieval motifs—the tower, pseudo-buttresses, and arched windows—were also minimal, but were important symbolic choices to reinforce the desired image. The "tower" and its motifs evoked the social and gastronomic prominence of royalty, just as "white"— the name as well as the building materials—evoked cleanliness and wholesomeness.

An exotic architectural theme was not an unusual choice for a commercial enterprise in the 1920s. An entrepreneur not only wanted his building to set the proper tone for his business. He also wanted it to catch the eye in an environment where neoclassical styles were generally reserved for civic buildings with medieval styles added for churches and schools. The new movie theaters led the scramble among the obscure and exotic styles, frequently appearing on main streets clothed in Moorish, Egyptian, or Mayan costumes while providing an equally exotic show inside on the screen. Since it was selling hamburgers and not fantasy, White Tower opted for a severely stripped version of a medieval fortress but packaged in a bold shape and clad in white glazed brick, an aggressively bright material whose surface and color had their own connotations.

While the interior of Milwaukee #1 made no references to the exterior's hint of medieval feasting, it did its best to fulfill all expectations of cleanliness and wholesomeness. The room was clean and simple (Fig. 2). The walls and ceiling were plastered and painted white, and the floor was tiled in the customer's area. Food was stored for the most part out of sight, and graphic display was confined to a framed menu on the rear wall. Five utilitarian stools along the counter gave Milwaukee #1 a limited capacity, and a basement provided limited space for storage and food preparation.

3. Milwaukee #5 (1927)

The grill was placed along the front counter by the entrance, where it was both easily visible and conveniently located for quick "carry out" service—an essential feature of a fast-food operation.

Although the White Towers were open twenty-four hours a day, seven days a week from the start, their menu was extremely limited. A hamburger weighed one ounce, was prepared to order in full view of the customer, and was served on a two-inch-diameter roll. It cost five cents. So did a freshly brewed cup of coffee. Donuts were served for breakfast, and ham sandwiches, pie, and soda pop were also available, but the hamburger made from reputable meat was the main attraction. The service was fast and friendly, but spartan. Countermen customarily greeted patrons as they entered, but everything was served on paper napkins. Mustard was available; ketchup was not.

Within two months after opening, the Saxes began to create their chain. The Siesel Construction Company started to build new shops, modeling them closely on Milwaukee #1, but Siesel was geared for large-scale projects like skyscrapers and theaters and not tiny White Towers. After building the first four White Towers, Siesel withdrew in favor of Charles Meier, a smaller Milwaukee contractor, who continued the expansion program. By the end of its first year the White Tower system had grown to half a dozen shops in Milwaukee and nearby Racine.

Meier made minor modifications to the original Siesel design, putting the tower in sharper relief and adding more decorative touches in the brickwork (Fig. 3), but the similarities of the White Towers far outweighed the differences. Furthermore, all of the towers were serving the same fare, which had been easily standardized because of its simplicity. Much of the food was supplied from a central commissary and delivered to the various shops in imaginative delivery trucks. The uniformity in the preparation of its food and the appearance of its buildings quickly built the White Tower chain's reputation for dependability. The signs on the shops now stressed "Hamburgers 5¢" and the company motto ("Buy a Bagfull") over the firm's name.

3

4. Detroit #26 (1929)

5. Minneapolis #2 (1929)

6. Detroit #27 (1929)

A year of operation had put the White Towers on solid footing, so the Saxes were ready to test the potential of their workingman's fast-food chain by risking a major expansion. Growth of some kind was inevitable, since volume is the key to profits in the fast-food business, and the Saxes "liked quick nickels better than slow quarters." Early in 1928 White Tower went to industrial Detroit and in one year built over thirty shops there. These Detroit White Towers were often tiny and crammed on tight sites (Fig. 4). Their budgets were also necessarily tight because of the ambitiousness of the expansion program, so towers were often built for less than $10,000 on land that was usually leased rather than purchased. The leasing of sites was an important technique that White Tower began to use successfully. By committing a minimum of its limited capital funds in land, the company was able to concentrate its assets on producing the maximum number of buildings. The Saxes knew that if the company could introduce a large number of towers around town, it would help to solidify its chain image, attract a clientele, and, of course, allow it to do more business and make more money. It was possible for a shop on a leased site to produce less income than a similar shop on a purchased site but still make a greater profit for the firm, since profit was measured as the return on the money invested. Furthermore, the lease arrangement was a good hedge against picking an unproductive location. The tiny White Towers were small enough to pick up and move to a more promising spot (Fig. 5), although just the threat of moving gave White Tower a strong bargaining position against a landlord trying to raise the rent. More important than financing arrangements, and even more important than architectural imagery, was the location and siting of these early Detroit shops. Locations near large factories were desirable, particularly when the factory worked more than one shift, since White Towers were open twenty-four hours a day (Fig. 6). Locating along major transit lines was equally desirable, especially at major transit interchanges or points of cross traffic (Fig. 7). Visibility was the key to siting, so corner locations became the most sought after, although just the impact of the white building on the street was almost as useful (Fig. 6).

7. Detroit #40 (1929)

8. Milwaukee #10 (1928)
9. Detroit #2 (1928)

10. Detroit #26 (1929)
11. Detroit #46 (1929)

Early in 1928 Clarence Haffeman, a burly builder and draftsman, had moved his family from Oklahoma to Detroit for the same reasons that the Saxes had brought the White Towers there—the booming automobile industry and the opportunities that it created. A few months after White Tower opened in Detroit, Haffeman was hired as the firm's building superintendent to organize and speed up its expansion program. First, he made a few changes to the basic Milwaukee design. Stepped pilasters were applied to the tower to give it more emphasis, and "medieval" crenelations were added to strengthen the building's profile (Figs. 8, 9). The residential sash windows were changed to plate glass topped off with a strip of leaded glass with "White Tower" decoratively set in it. Haffeman then drew up a basic set of plans in two versions—"righthand" and "lefthand"—to accommodate any site orientation (Figs. 10, 11). Next he organized three building crews of carpenters and masons, each of which operated as a team. As soon as a new site was found and leased, one of the building crews was ready to start. Two weeks later all the restaurant equipment arrived for installation. The equipment had been ordered in advance and custom-made by the Sewers Restaurant Equipment Company in Detroit. Essentially Haffeman created for White Towers what Henry Ford had created for automobiles—a production line that could produce new White Towers at the rate of one a week.

Production-line efficiency was management's goal for all aspects of the quickly growing chain. In February 1929 Arnold Saxe, T. E. Saxe's cousin, came to White Tower from the Saxe Theaters (a move from the fifth to the third floors in the Wisconsin Theater Building in Milwaukee) to help organize and coordinate the day-to-day operations. Food purchasing procedures were rationalized, and equipment was analyzed with respect to simplified procedures behind the counter. Now a change in the menu would produce a coordinated response from the sign shop.

The Detroit gamble proved a success. The Saxes had developed the right formula, which combined a limited menu of wholesome food with speedy service, packaged in imageful buildings that were shrewdly placed and efficiently managed. In the next year the

5

12. Philadelphia #1 (1930)
13. Boston #2 (1931)

14. Rochester #2 (1932)
15. Washington #2 (1932)

16. Philadelphia #9 (1932)

17. Milwaukee #1 (1929)

18. Milwaukee #1 (1926)
19. Milwaukee #1 (1929)

depression made everyone a White Tower customer, and success was assured.

In the early years of the depression, White Tower continued to expand aggressively following J. E. Saxe's dictum: "If you don't build in slow times, you can't be ready for good times." "In those years there was a depression, but we went ahead. I talked to big developers and they would say to me, 'White Tower must have a lot of nerve, spending money now. I'm going to hold back.' I said, 'Well, don't hold back too much, you never know.'" By now the elder Saxe had sold his movie theaters and was working for White Tower full time. His forte was real estate, and he was constantly on the road looking for suitable locations for new towers. Glazed-brick White Towers in the Detroit style were appearing with increasing frequency in the urban centers to the east, in Cleveland, Pittsburgh, Philadelphia, New York, Boston, Providence, and Washington, as Haffeman and his crews took to the road (Figs. 12–15). In 1932, White Tower shifted its headquarters from Milwaukee to Pittsburgh to be more central to its growing chain.

Moving into larger cities meant both bigger crowds of potential customers along the street and higher ground rents to match, so Haffeman enlarged his basic design, providing ten to twelve stools rather than five or six, to promote a higher volume of trade on both accounts (Fig. 16). While his crews worked their way eastward building new shops, Haffeman started a parallel program of systematic renovation of the older ones. He bought sheets of porcelain enamel from the Wolverine Company in Detroit and started installing them in the early plastered interiors, which were particularly vulnerable to wear and hard to clean. Fittingly, one of the first shops to be renovated was Milwaukee #1. It was also the first shop to be moved when the landlord wanted its corner site for a gas station. After moving it halfway along the block, Haffeman expanded the original shop to the rear, doubling its capacity and providing an adequate back room (Fig. 17). He then reclad the interior in porcelain enamel, replaced the double-hung windows with plate glass, and attached an elaborate, neon-illuminated sign to the tower to compensate for the reduced visibility of the mid-block location (Figs. 18, 19). The most significant change was the

6

20. New York #1 (1930)

21. Philadelphia #9 (1932)

22. Boston #1 (1932)

23. New York #11 (1933)
24. Boston #8 (1932)

addition of gooseneck lamps. Up to this point White Tower had found existing street lighting adequate to illuminate its buildings at night. In this case, Milwaukee #1 had been moved from under a streetlight into the shadows, forcing White Tower to provide its own lighting. The gooseneck lamps transformed the tower into an oasis of light at night and were quickly installed throughout the chain (Fig. 20).

In both their location and siting the new towers showed the Saxes' attention to their basic principles. In Philadelphia, for instance, White Tower #9 was placed next to the steps of the new Race-Vine Subway Station, across the street from Town Hall Auditorium and two blocks from City Hall (Fig. 21). By 1932 more than half of the stations along the Broad Street Subway had White Towers near the top of their steps, convenient to the users of the subway and the connecting trolley and bus lines.

Vacant land was at a premium in the large eastern cities, so White Tower often found it difficult to acquire open sites where it wanted them. In many cases it was forced to rent space in existing buildings or to accept storefronts in the middle of blocks to secure good locations. Since the White Tower ideal was "a well-illuminated individual building having a corner location (Fig. 22)" it was always a compromise for White Tower to apply its facade on an existing building. When faced with these situations, White Tower searched for architectural devices that would give its shops the illusion, at least, of an individual building. The contrast between the bright white glazed-brick facade and the darker building to which it was attached would always make the White Tower stand out, but the effect could be enhanced. At New York #11, for instance, the tower was disengaged from the building behind it and allowed to slide past the windows of the second floor (Fig. 23). At Boston #8 the masonry surrounding the applied facade was painted black to emphasize the illusion of an individual building (Fig. 24). Difficult sites would be a constant challenge for White Tower designers, because good locations in any form and busy corners in particular were the company's first priority, and J. E. was concentrating on finding them where he could. "A building . . . could be under

7

25. Philadelphia #3 (1930)

26. Rochester #1 (1931)

27. Window stickers

construction and there might be a sign on it saying 'corner for lease.' J. E. would be there to pick up the corner."

The depression not only provided White Tower with its clientele, it also provided the firm with a willing, inexpensive labor force (Fig. 25). "When I got my job in New York there must have been fifty guys on the stairway waiting to come in." Thankful for their jobs, White Tower men worked long hours, and under the watchful eyes of the store manager, kept the buildings immaculately clean inside and out. "Guys like Bernie Gooch used to put toothpicks in the corner of the refrigerator to see whether you'd cleaned it or not. It didn't make a difference how clean it was. If the toothpick was there you hadn't cleaned it." The interiors were entirely washed down twice a week by the night shift, and the exteriors once a week by the day shift. The windows were washed every day. The building not only had to be clean, it had to look clean. "The tower could be slightly dirty on the inside or outside, but if the windows were clean it always looked good." An esprit de corps developed among the employees and was fostered by management. A weekly newsletter, *Tower Topics*, kept up a steady stream of company contests, helpful hints, and encouragement.

The White Tower clientele continued to match its staff—working-class men (Fig. 26)—and, as a result, White Towers quickly developed a reputation as all-male preserves. Of course management tried to encourage female patronage. "We started putting booths in the towers for the ladies to come in and sit down." Women behind the counter were helpful in this regard. "Girls got more women to come in. In fact, we used to have signs on the windows—ladies invited—because it was hard to get women to come in." But girls behind the counter were rare. "During the thirties women didn't work. They were home. It wasn't the thing for a girl to work."

After five years of operation T. E. Saxe set out to raise the level of service and expand the menu to provide the necessary variety for twenty-four-hour service. Plates and silverware were added. In addition to the basic hamburger, coffee, and donut fare, the sandwich selection was expanded with some local variations (Fig. 27). For example, chili and chow mein were popular in Detroit. The

28. Philadelphia #8 (1932)

29. New York #10 (1933)

30. New York #10 (1933)

expansion of the menu required an expansion of storage and preparation space in the White Towers, and a larger dishwashing area was required for the plates and silverware. In accommodating these demands the new White Towers had to be somewhat larger and therefore more expensive, so management had to expect more business from the new shops in return. When the towers were in good locations, the twenty-four-hour menu successfully provided increased business to compensate for the added expenses.

Along with the expansion of the menu came an important shift of emphasis in the White Tower image from the "Medieval Tower," symbolizing royalty and social and gastronomic prominence, to the "Modern Tower," symbolizing luxury, cleanliness, speed, and efficiency. The catalyst for the change came from an unusual source—a new building material, procelain enamel. White glazed bricks had served the company's functional and symbolic needs adequately for more than seven years, but White Tower management never liked using them. The mortar joints made the surfaces hard to clean, and they often needed repointing. Furthermore, glazed brick was in short supply on the East Coast in the early 1930s. White Tower had been using porcelain enamel sheets in all of its interiors for some time (Fig. 28), but the idea of using them outside was entirely a different matter, since techniques for joining and waterproofing them had not been completely developed. As early as 1929, however, White Tower had begun to experiment with reflective sheet materials like Vitrolite in an effort to achieve a brighter effect that was also easier to clean and maintain. In 1933 the Saxes, who were always interested in trying new ideas, accepted a proposal from the Vitrolite Company to design and build a new White Tower to show what their product could do. The Vitrolite shop, New York #10, was bright, elegant, and lavish in its use of materials both inside and out (Fig. 29, 30). Vitrolite panels in various shades were trimmed in stainless steel and decorated with glass inserts and terra-cotta copings. White Tower was delighted with the building's appearance ("In the daytime it was beautiful, and at night it was better") but not its cost. Furthermore, Vitrolite, a colored opaque glass, was brittle and easily cracked. However, New York #10, in an indirect way,

9

31. Syracuse #1 (1934)

32. Philadelphia #5 (1930)
33. New York #13 (1934)

34. Rochester #2 (1932)
35. Syracuse #1 (1933)

36. Syracuse #1 (1933)
37. Rochester #5 (1936)

38. New York #13 (1934)

encouraged the development of the techniques for using the less expensive and more durable porcelain enamel panels on the White Tower facades. A Syracuse businessman, Bill Mahoney, saw the Vitrolite White Tower soon after it was built and was struck by its appearance. He decided to have a porcelain enamel version of it built in Syracuse, where he would go into the hamburger business himself. His builder did such a good job that the Saxes made him a generous offer for his shop. Mahoney, who knew nothing about operating a restaurant, sold his building to White Tower while it was still under construction, 75 percent complete. Haffeman finished the shop as Syracuse #1 (Fig. 31) and then used it as the basis for White Tower's new style of building. Mahoney's builder had solved the technical problems of using porcelain enamel by strapping the sheets in place with a good number of stainless-steel strips, which masked the uneven joints and provided visual sparkle as well.

Like Vitrolite, porcelain enamel had a generally brighter and cleaner effect than glazed brick (Figs. 32, 33), and it looked better when illuminated at night. The new porcelain enamel shops were obviously modern, because the material itself carried that connotation. They also appeared more luxurious, since new ornamental touches now flourished in the form of pale green pilasters on the tower and corners, floral panels, door pulls, and pilaster caps. Even the hamburger sign, now baked into a porcelain panel, became a decorative motif. "In those days the more 'gingerbread' there was the more luxurious it was. A big theatrical designer in New York mentioned that they make theaters gracious and glorious so that when a person pays his buck and a half admission he feels that he half owns it and he's in a palace. Now back in those days it was a similar thing for us. The more metal that was on . . . actually people asked us if Andrew Mellon was behind White Tower." The whole effect was perhaps a bit too rich, since some of the stylish touches detracted from the building's overall impact. The pale green pilasters, in particular, emphasized the corners at the expense of the building as a whole, so they were reclad in white. Now a porcelain enamel White Tower looked as if a glazed-brick tower had been dressed overnight in a new outfit (Figs. 34, 35).

39. Food display

40. Paterson #1 (1935)

41. Milwaukee #10 (1928)
42. Boston #2 (1931)

43. Hartford #1 (1935)
44. New York #15 (1935)

It is significant to note at this point that the interior and exterior of the building were now clad in the same material, so that the patron's visual expectations were literally fulfilled as he entered the shop (Figs. 36, 37). The larger plate-glass windows of the new towers attempted to exploit this connection by allowing the passer-by a better view in. With the interior-to-exterior relationship made more explicit, it was clearly necessary to make the interiors more crisp and jazzy in parallel. Backs were added to the stools, making them more comfortable, and expensive shining materials were used everywhere in strong decorative arrangements (Fig. 38). Porcelain enamel, glazed tile, and stainless steel sparkled in the light and played off against the food on display and on the plate. The massed display of food whetted the appetite and complemented the the elaborated menu and message boards. *Tower Topics* illustrated various display layouts. "The big deal was mass displays. That was our theory. If you have one piece of pie up there you'll never sell it. Put ten or twelve pies up there and you'll sell it (Fig. 39)." The Saxes did not mind the extra expense of the building because it paid off in the long run. "Build well to eliminate maintenance" was the motto. After all, White Tower's primary form of advertising was the striking appearance of its buildings.

By 1935 the White Tower chain had grown to more than 130 towers stretching over 1100 miles from Boston to Minneapolis. Building and renovating shops all over the country was keeping Haffeman on the road for days on end. The increased travel was putting a strain on his large family, so he was ready to resign his position. Out of necessity, and partly because they liked to test new ideas, the Saxes began to hire a variety of local architects and builders to do their work. The architects were mostly modest local practitioners, but occasionally White Tower would hire a nationally recognized designer like B. Sumner Gruzen, who designed the elegant Paterson #1 in 1935 (Fig. 40). However, different architects meant different stylistic results (Figs. 41–44) and occasionally a lack of skill in handling the very specific requirements of kitchen equipment and stringent health codes, so the overall result of this procedure was not satisfactory to the firm. The chain needed a consistent style connected to the use of its new material, and the first generation of brick buildings needed to be systematically remodeled—reclad to

45. Baltimore #3 (1936)

46. New York #13 (1934)
47. New York #18 (1936)

48. Philadelphia #1 (1930)
49. Philadelphia #1 (1939)

50. Boston #1 (1931)
51. Boston #1 (1938)

52. Providence #3 (1937)

look the same as the porcelain enamel buildings and renovated to accommodate new equipment. White Tower also needed to maintain a thread of consistency as the range of site conditions and the number of resultant building types expanded. White Tower needed a staff architect.

In November 1935 White Tower advertised for an architect in the New York newspapers. One of many who responded was Charles J. Johnson, an architect with twelve years of experience in large New York architectural offices, who for the past three years had been able to find work only as a surveyor. A week after responding to the ad, Johnson got an evening phone call from J. E. Saxe asking him to come to the White Tower office at once for an interview. When Johnson arrived, J. E. was ready to fire all sorts of questions at him. Johnson fielded the questions smartly, so J. E. offered him the job. Johnson was not at all sure what he was getting into ("What did I know about the restaurant business?") but he took the job ("After all, people always have to eat."). He began work in the small office above New York #13, which doubled as the New York commissary and J. E. Saxe's base for real estate operations. The job was demanding from the start, since J. E. had fifteen new leases in hand and needed designs for them. Johnson had to work nights to keep up, but his energy and imagination were equal to the task.

At the start Johnson's designs set out in more than one direction. First, he modified the current porcelain enamel tower design by replacing the fussy, decorative, stainless-steel details with simpler plates and strips and thinning the black enamel base (Fig. 45). In one stroke he was able to abstract in a modern vocabulary the literal medieval imagery that remained on the earlier porcelain enamel towers and thus provide a smooth transition toward White Tower's new style (Figs. 46, 47). Johnson's simplified porcelain enamel design also fit easily over the bumps and steps of the brick towers, and the resulting modifications were almost indistinguishable from the new buildings (Figs. 48–51). This was the desired result, since the switch from glazed brick to porcelain enamel had given the White Tower chain a split identity. These renovations were actively pursued in the late 1930s even though most of the brick towers were less than seven years old and in good structural condition.

12

53. Paterson #1 (1935)

54. New York #17 (1936)

55. Plan of Camden #2 (1937)

56. Camden #2 (1937)

Next Johnson discarded all remnants of the medieval White Towers and started to experiment boldly in the streamlined Moderne style that was in vogue with commercial designers at the time (Fig. 52). Its insistence on the aerodynamic imagery of speed and movement was consistent with the subject matter of gas stations and fast food. Johnson's designs employed the basic streamlined motifs—bold horizontals, curved corners, maximum glass area—which easily conveyed the message of cleanliness, speed, and modernity when executed in porcelain enamel and stainless steel. But the tower design, stripped of its medieval imagery, was mainly decorative and looked weak and awkward on a corner.

Johnson's temperament and design sensibilities were particularly suited for the role of a company architect. His designs could be characterized as an economical expression of the practical and symbolic needs of the company. As he said, "It wasn't so much the aesthetics of it. We're in business to make a buck." To illustrate this approach it is worth comparing Johnson's streamlined White Towers with Gruzen's Paterson #1, which was clearly one of Johnson's inspirations for his streamlined designs (Figs. 53, 54). Gruzen's beautiful design pressed the architectural notions of horizontality and continuity to their ultimate expressions, often using expensive and difficult details to maintain the consistency of the architectural idea. Johnson's design, while not as striking as Paterson #1, stressed the same general effects of horizontality and continuity but sought to achieve them in a manner that was both economical and easy to maintain. So where Paterson #1 had large sheets of specially curving glass precariously butt-jointed (Fig. 53), New York #17 firmly strapped together standard sizes of glass in aluminum frames (Fig. 54).

During the mid-1930s White Tower was attracted to the possibilities of placing White Towers on major roadways so they could serve customers who traveled in automobiles as well as on trolleys and subways. In his first months on the job Johnson designed a new building type not much larger than the city towers (it provided only seven stools plus window counters) but specifically tailored for open sites along highways (Figs. 55, 56). Its steel frame construction allowed for a large sweep of uninterrupted glass, which helped to

13

57. Camden #4 (1938)

58. Buffalo #1A (1938)

59. New York #19 (1936)

scale the building to the moving automobile. The large, curved corners, which were a particularly effective aspect of the design for emphasizing the scale of the large windows, were not the architect's idea. "The owner of White Tower insisted on a rounded corner. Well, I thought that would be too expensive. He asked, 'Will the rounded corners be expensive?' I said yes, and he asked, 'Will they be so expensive that other people may not be able to afford them?' When I said, 'It might be,' he said, 'Then I want them.' "

The roadside shops were placed close to the highway so they would be easily seen (Fig. 57). Johnson had located the entrance and tower in the center of the building, making them equally visible to traffic moving in either direction, but, unlike the windows, the tower was not scaled to the road, so it looked small in relation to the building as a whole. In fact, the tower had been aesthetically adrift since the medieval motifs and their symbolic connotations had been removed. It was clearly useful as an entrance marker, but the fact that "tower" was part of the company's name was more to the point. It was assuredly the company symbol for better or worse, so it had to be improved. "We were somewhat criticized for our tower so Mr. J. E. asked me, 'Now, what's the reason for the tower?' He said the tower wasn't functional. I said, 'I'll tell you how we can make the tower functional. We'll put a clock up there' " (Fig. 56). The clock tower was a popular commercial motif at the time, was certainly a generous civic gesture, and might have satisfied J. E. Saxe's uneasiness about the tower's function, but it did not really provide support for hamburger salesmanship or White Tower imagery. The tower of the roadside design was subsequently enlarged, and two years later, at Buffalo #1A, it finally came, clockless, into balance with both the highway alongside and the building below, tied more firmly to its base, with its decoration making emphatic the use of the tower as a marker of the entrance below (Fig. 58).

Before White Tower fully understood how to run a roadside operation, a number of operational experiments would be necessary. In addition to the normal counter service inside, the first roadside towers had slide-up windows by the griddle for "carry out" supplemented by carhops for curb service (Fig. 59). However, the

14

60. Camden #5 (1936)

61. New York #23 (1937)

62. Camden #5 (1936)

63. New York #19 (1936)

slide-up window proved awkward and was abandoned in favor of carhop curb service alone. Johnson had seen other roadside restaurants trying to serve their carhops through the front door, but the congestion caused by the regular customers made this system inefficient and awkward. So a separate curb station with its own griddle was installed in the back room of Camden #2. It was a tight fit, but proved efficient. It had to be, because curb service proved to be enormously popular. "Fifty-six hamburgers got on that griddle every three minutes and fifty-six went out the window."

Of all the roadside towers—over a dozen of them built from 1936 to 1939—Camden #5 was the most unusual because White Tower had not built it. Local entrepreneurs built it in 1936 at almost exactly the time White Tower was opening its first roadside shop in Elizabeth, New Jersey, and over a year before White Tower ventured into suburban Camden. The window openings of Camden #5 were curved on either end in the characteristic manner of the Cushman Bakery chain of New York. Otherwise, it had a central tower and entrance, large, wrap-around windows, white porcelain enamel cladding, gooseneck lamps, and a tiled interior (Fig. 60), so it was almost identical to a roadside White Tower, both inside and out (Figs. 60, 61). When the Camden entrepreneurs decided to start a White Tower type of hamburger shop they naturally borrowed its buildings' characteristics as well. Whether it was true or not, the entrepreneurs perceived the business and the building to be inseparable and equal game for their initiative. In some of the detailed aspects of its design, however, Camden #5 was better adapted to its highway site than its White Tower contemporaries. The mass of its tower was in proportion to the building and in scale with the road. The building had been consistently conceived and executed in the streamlined style, while White Towers still retained vestigial touches of the medieval in the vertical fluting around the tower and on the corners. The corner fluting was especially in conflict with the character of the building, since visually it interrupted the sweeping effect of the curved corner. Camden #5, on the other hand, followed the idea of the sweeping corner to its most rigorous architectural conclusion by using every possible device to eliminate intrusions on the effect.

15

64. New York #24 (1938)

65. Window stickers

66. Moving New York #6A

The curved glass was butt-jointed and held in place with tiny clips, while the corner was actually supported by the slenderest of lally columns set well back from the building's surface (Figs. 60, 62). In comparison the White Towers tiptoed cautiously around the curving corner. The glass was subdivided and firmly framed in place, and the supporting column, although quite slender, came to the face of the building once the corner had been turned (Figs. 61, 63). In the end, however, competition in the fast-food business centered less on the subtleties of a building's image on the roadside than it did on the quality, price, and service of the hamburgers on the plate. In 1941, after only five years in business, the Camden entrepreneurs sold their shop to White Tower, and, with only the addition of a new sign, it continued in operation as Camden #5.

In the late 1930s and early 1940s White Tower broadened its experiments with its menu to keep the interest of steady customers, who formed the bulk of its clientele. It introduced its first printed menu and added more sandwiches. It also experimented with ice cream, which was, in this case, a soft custard prepared in batches on the premises. Signs promoted it heavily, especially in connection with the roadside towers (Figs. 64, 65), but it varied in texture from batch to batch and, although it was high in quality, it never caught on. On the other hand, bacon and eggs were immediately popular when they joined coffee and donuts on the breakfast menu. Although the variety of the menu might have been helpful in appealing to steady customers, its composition was a critical factor for the basic business barometer—profits. Building costs had been escalating in the late thirties, and White Tower had been consciously building with expensive materials to achieve a desired image and to conform to strict building and health codes. As building costs rose, the firm needed to increase gross returns to maintain its margin of profit. Volume had already been maximized, since White Tower had always been open twenty-four hours a day and the menu had been expanded to cover the full daily cycle of meals. In addition, the Saxes had been very skillful in finding busy locations for their towers and had occasionally moved buildings when their locations proved unprofitable (Fig. 66). The next step for White Tower was to upgrade its product to increase both the price and potential profit on each item sold.

67. Camden #3 (1938)

68. Camden #3 (1938)

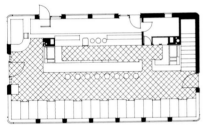

69. Plan of Camden #3 (1938)

70. Silver Spring #1 (1938)

71. Silver Spring #1 (1938)

Toward the end of 1937 Johnson was directed to develop a new deluxe White Tower for the roadside, twice as big as normal White Towers with three times as many seats. This White Tower could really be called a restaurant, with its booth seating, varied menu, and, for the first time, a ten-cent hamburger. The first deluxe tower was built in Camden across the road from Camden #2 and was called Marbett's (a combination of the names of T. E. Saxe's sisters, Margaret and Betty) to keep the illusion of direct competition (Fig. 67). Even its curb service was deluxe. A platoon of girl carhops, jauntily uniformed like movie palace usherettes, were commanded by a supervisor who patrolled the parking area on roller skates (Fig. 68) The curb service had been cleverly worked into the well-organized plan. The carhops had their own entrance and exit but shared the back counter and griddle with the countermen. A single cashier served both the carhops and the customers who ate inside (Fig. 69). Those who left their cars entered a dining room that had reached the apex of White Tower elegance in cool porcelain enamel, bright stainless steel, and jazzy tile (Fig. 70). To make the exterior of this streamlined palace, Johnson added a strong horizontal accent in the form of a stainless steel, neon-edged canopy which surrounded the basic porcelain enamel box while containing and concealing the exterior lighting fixtures. On the well-proportioned tower Johnson applied a series of vertical fin accents closely modeled on the tower of Paterson #1. "We did a little cribbing here and there. I cribbed from one store to another."

The deluxe towers in Camden and Silver Spring, Maryland, were successful in resolving the problem of visibility along the roadside. The tower was no longer just a symbol. With the addition of a streamlined, cantilevered, neon-illuminated "restaurant" sign it was also a signpost. At the urging of J. E. Saxe (who loved signs) the facades above the canopy were eventually covered with all sorts of signs, applied and illuminated, making the whole building a sign, a signpost, and more the image of speed and modernity on the parking lot than the cars around it (Fig. 71).

The deluxe White Towers may have been an aesthetic success along the roadside, but they were not an economic success. The extra expense of a big building on a big site serving an extensive menu

17

72. Washington #2A (1940)

73. Washington #2A (1940)

74. Paterson #1 (1945)

75. Philadelphia #17 (1954)

failed to produce the increased trade that was hoped for. Perhaps White Tower's clientele just was not ready for the ten-cent hamburger. In any case, the deluxe restaurant experiment was abandoned, and White Tower again concentrated on medium-sized buildings serving its standard fare.

The architectural lessons of the deluxe towers were not abandoned, however. Their signpost and streamlining themes were refined in Johnson's designs for Washington #2A (Fig. 72). The windows were enlarged and their frames diminished, giving a big scale and curtain-wall openness to the long wall. Stainless-steel trim was concentrated in the bold horizontal of the canopy (borrowed directly from the deluxe towers), which made emphatic the division between the windows and doors below and the porcelain enamel and tower above. For the first time the tower was used purely as a signpost with the words "White Tower" placed on it in stylish, three-dimensional letters that Johnson had designed himself. The letters were large, almost three feet high, and, like the building itself, made in white porcelain enamel, but they were outlined with narrow black channels, which gave them an illuminated quality that was legible at some distance up and down the street (Fig. 73). The tower-as-signpost theme was to become an important element in all of Johnson's postwar designs, since Washington #2A had demonstrated that it was applicable to downtown sites as well as roadside sites.

By 1940 the greatest concentration of White Towers was in the large eastern cities, and the most active areas for expansion were toward the Northeast, in the smaller industrial cities there, and toward the South, below Washington. White Tower again felt the pressure to relocate its headquarters closer to the center of the chain, and so in April 1941 the main office was moved from Pittsburgh to Stamford, Connecticut, where management had found an elegant, neo-Georgian building for sale.

Just as the depression had given White Tower its labor force, World War II abruptly took it away, as men were drawn into the armed forces. White Tower, which had used women as carhops and occasionally as waitresses, now was forced to use them almost

18

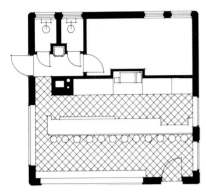

76. Plan of a "bread and butter"

77. Baltimore #6 (1941)

78. Dayton #3 (1941)

exclusively behind the counters of its workingman's restaurants (Fig. 74). "Before the war they didn't work. They were home. During the war, when the boys went into the army, the wives went out and worked to subsidize the husband's salary." Perhaps this change had an effect on the team feeling of the staff or on the working-class-male image of the White Tower operation, but it was more a signal for major postwar economic problems for T. E. Saxe. In the wartime and postwar economy there was plenty of work, at better pay and shorter hours than White Tower had become accustomed to offering its countermen. Now only women were available for counter jobs, and White Tower had to pay more for their services (Fig. 75). Rising labor costs also meant rising costs of construction and, in the general climate of postwar expansion, rising real estate costs as well. During its first twenty years of operation, White Tower had been able to manipulate its basic cost variables—construction, real estate, labor, and food—to its advantage. Now all these variables combined to squeeze profits. Saxe had already expanded the menu to the capacity of his buildings and had experimented with an upgraded product in the deluxe towers. Now he relied on the twenty years' experience of his staff to make all aspects of White Tower operation more efficient.

Just before World War II effectively put a stop to new construction, Johnson had come up with his "bread and butter" design. It was almost the same size as the roadside towers (twenty-five feet by twenty-six feet versus twenty-five by twenty-five), but its internal arrangement was more efficient (seating twelve compared to seven in the roadside towers with more window shelf space as well), thus providing for a higher volume of business for the same building cost (Figs. 76, 77). The griddle was moved from its symbolic location near the entrance to a more efficient spot in the center of the back counter. Even the stools became more utilitarian by losing their backrests. "I was talking to a very successful individual in Washington and he said, 'You people are silly having backs on the stools. Customers stay there too long.'" In keeping with its efficient plan the "bread and butter" design eliminated the costly curved corners that Johnson had always considered unnecessary and limited stainless-steel trim to just a few horizontal strips (Fig. 78). The "bread and butter" returned the tower to the corner of the building

19

79. Boston #2 (1931)
80. Baltimore #8 (1948)

81. Norfolk #3A (1965)

82. Philadelphia #14 (1947)

83. Riverdale #1 (1953)

84. New York #13 (1954)
85. Norfolk #34 (1956)

like most earlier towers, so, except for a larger expanse of glass, they had a similar appearance (Figs. 79, 80). However, the tower itself, a smoothly modeled version of the glazed-brick design, took a curious step backward from an advertising point of view by being left bare, and not being used as a signboard.

When building resumed after the war Johnson began with "bread and butters" but soon developed them into the postwar style that was to serve White Tower extraordinarily well for almost twenty more years. With more than fifteen years' experience, White Tower's porcelain enamel fabricators had improved their techniques of fastening and joining panels so that strips of stainless steel were no longer required to hide inaccuracies. Johnson was now able to refine a White Tower to its purest abstract form—a simple white cube (Fig. 81). The use of steel framing and air conditioning allowed for large expanses of fixed plate glass, which emphasized the building's giant scale that was so effective in relating them to the highway and in providing impact in built-up areas. In some cases the windows seemed to cover more than half of the building's surface, but they did not detract from the impact of the overall cubic form or the effect of whiteness, since the interiors were as white as the exterior (Fig. 82). At night, the glow from the windows actually provided additional exterior illumination as well as an enticing view in. Finally, and most important, the tower was once again both a symbol and a signpost. Johnson's "White Tower" sign was graphically improved by an advertising consultant's suggestion to connect horizontal strokes to the *W* and the *T*. The stylish, black-outlined "White Tower" logo was then placed redundantly on the actual white tower, and the leitmotif of "hamburgers" (banished from the signs in the forties when the price rose about five cents) returned as a subtitle above the windows (Fig. 83). "We still liked the word 'hamburgers.' Hamburgers, we think, bring in the business." The pure cube style, the ultimate in porcelain-enamel technology and billboard efficiency, was the ultimate solution for chain consistency, since it made renovations ((Fig. 84) indistinguishable from new buildings (Fig. 85). Furthermore, by emphasizing signs, glass, and the pure form of the building while de-emphasizing explicit decorative touches, hints of richness, and the imagery of speed, the pure cube

86. Stamford #2 (1951)
87. A Valentine sandwich shop

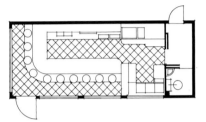

88. Plan of Richmond #5 (1950)

89. Richmond #5 (1950)

style was keeping White Tower in step with general postwar architectural trends toward abstraction.

Perhaps the most successful of the pure cube buildings were the fifteen prefabricated towers built by the Valentine Manufacturing Company of Wichita, Kansas. Johnson modified the basic Valentine frame, which was used for houses and motel units as well as stores, into the most efficient White Tower ever built (Figs. 86, 87). In this ten-foot-by-twenty-five-foot building, no larger than some of the early Detroit towers, he managed to fit ten stools plus all the equipment and storage space necessary for White Tower's 1950 bill of fare (Fig. 88). The Valentine Company fabricated the steel shell for Johnson's plan and window arrangement and sent it to the site, where the foundation and utilities had been prepared. White Tower arranged for erection of the tower and the porcelain enamel cladding. The resulting White Towers bore no resemblance to the manufacturer's prototypes (Figs. 86, 87). These "Valentines" were as efficient visually as they were functionally (Fig. 89). Their towers were overlarge and pushed to one end. The openings were proportionally very large, and, combined with the simple large graphics, gave these tiny buildings a gigantic scale. The effect of a six-foot man sitting inside a building less than nine feet high was startling to the point of perceptual trickery (Fig. 90). These little but big buildings were the perfect combination of tower symbol for recognition, large-scale window openings for highway impact, and bold graphics to reinforce the message—hamburgers. These characteristics made the Valentines suitable for any potential White Tower site. They were small enough to fit in the tightest urban spots while maintaining the visual impact needed for open highway sites. Being prefabricated, the Valentines had ease of transport built into them, although moving towers to better locations was rarely economically feasible after the war, and only one was actually moved. Their real value to the company was the operational efficiency of their tight plan (Fig. 91) and the economy of their construction. Valentines, originally planned to give ten years of service, are still in use after twenty-five years.

The White Tower chain benefited from the postwar prosperity, reaching its largest numerical expansion in the mid-1950s, when it

21

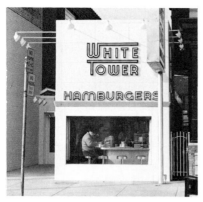

90. Philadelphia #17 (1954)

91. Stamford #2 (1951)

was operating over 230 shops. By the early 1960s, however, the pinch of rising costs, changing eating habits, and, most important, competition from a new generation of hamburger chains led by McDonald's, warned that the era of the workingman's restaurant, the made-to-order hamburger, and the shining white tower was almost over. White Tower knew as well as McDonald's that the hamburger market of the sixties and seventies was in the suburbs along the commercial strip, but the majority of White Tower locations, chosen up to thirty years before, were in decaying downtown areas and tied to trolley and bus lines that no longer carried the majority of potential White Tower customers. White Tower's reputation—a considerable source of pride carefully nurtured over the years—was tarnished by the unattractive context in which their shops now appeared and with which they began to be associated. More to the point was the fact that labor and food costs now demanded five times the sales volume of the 1930s to make the older locations profitable, so White Tower was forced to consolidate and abandon its marginal shops. Conditions favored a large national organization that could take advantage of economies of scale. Where White Tower had always been a family-run company, first local and then regional in scope, McDonald's had become a giant, multinational franchising corporation, operating in 1977 almost twenty times the number of shops that White Tower had at its peak in the 1950s.

There was also the question of changing social patterns. Where White Tower had tied hamburgers to public transportation and the workingman, with no advertising other than the appearance of its buildings and the quality of its food, McDonald's tied hamburgers to the car, children, and the family with large doses of child-related national advertising and promotion. White Tower had always prepared its hamburgers in full view and made to order for each customer as visible proof of food quality. By the 1960s food purity was no longer a major issue for the customer, and McDonald's precooked and packaged convenience foods were cheaper and always ready to go. If people could assume that health standards were always observed, then the image of cleanliness and purity of the shining white building itself was no longer critical. It was even questionable whether or not the shining white building still evoked

92. Atlantic City #2 (1955)
93. Milwaukee #2A (1950)

94. Albany #2 (1962)
95. Richmond #5 (1950)

96. Baltimore #9 (1957)

97. Rochester #2B (1965)

that image. The streamlined Moderne, after all, was no longer "modern" in the public eye, so White Tower now felt obliged to tinker with the appearance of its buildings. In 1956 White Tower used color on its buildings for the first time in twenty-five years when it changed its signs from white outlined in black to orange and turquoise, similar to, but not quite the same as, the Howard Johnson's colors. Eye-catching neon and rear-illuminated signs were added to White Towers with increasing frequency. At first the signs maintained an architectural relationship to the buildings like the few white porcelain enamel signs that were cantilevered off towers in response to particularly difficult site conditions (Fig. 92). Subsequently the signs grew larger and more responsive to billboard priorities than to architectural criteria (Fig. 93). Most were made freestanding and mounted on a pole by the curb (Fig. 95), but those attached to the front or the top of White Towers were particularly insensitive to the buildings in scale, material, proportion, and placement (Fig. 94). Signs may have become the basic manner of business identification, especially on the highway, but in its use of them White Tower was betraying a lack of confidence in the ability of the shining white building (Fig. 96) to carry the company's message. In the mid-sixties Johnson did a series of skillful renovations, which featured a large-scale, back-illuminated sign wrapped around the top of the building (Fig. 97). The tower, however, was no longer white, but was decorated with a series of blue and white vertical stripes (Fig. 97)! After the "white" disappeared, the "tower" soon followed in a series of curtain-wall designs that replaced the tower with a cantilevered sign (Fig. 98). After forty years of use, the white tower was no longer considered mandatory as the company's symbol. The mansarded, suburban residential style had taken over as the accepted genre for fast-food eateries (Fig. 99).

In January 1977, White Tower, in conjunction with its fiftieth anniversary, changed its corporate name to Tombrock, reflecting the fact that it had become a diversified food service organization under the direction of Brock Saxe, T. E.'s son, who had taken over as president of White Tower when his father retired in 1970. Tombrock still profitably operates over eighty White Towers today. In addition, the corporation operates Brocks, a steakhouse chain

98. Atlantic City #3 (1965)

99. Raleigh #2 (1972)

100. Truck (1929)

faithfully modeled on Irish pubs and aimed at the suburban business and adult dining market. Since 1975 the corporation has operated Burger Kings in the Washington area and Golden Skillet Chicken units in Richmond, Virginia, under franchise agreements—a logical response to today's fast-food market by an organization with a wealth of experience in the field.

The hamburger business today is clearly dominated by the golden arches of McDonald's. It is interesting to note that to reach that position McDonald's has seemed to follow the same strategies that White Tower used in the preceding generation. Both chains started when an entrepreneur saw an opportunity to sell a limited product in a distinctive building with a distinctive symbol placed in convenient locations. Both chains profited from the availability of cheap labor and a sound knowledge of real estate. When their idea caught hold, both entrepreneurs took a big risk to expand their chain. When, because of fortuitous circumstances, their expansion was successful, both chains moved to diversify their product to provide for the daily cycle of meals and to offer variety to their steady customers. At a time when both chains were firmly established, both radically changed their buildings' basic appearance and image, but did not suffer from it. In time, both diversified their locations. Where White Tower moved from downtown to the suburban roadside, McDonald's moved from the commercial strip back downtown, and then overseas.

While the development of the second generation of hamburger chains may be difficult to predict, the model for their development is clear. For over fifty years White Towers from Milwaukee to New York and from Boston to Tampa have acquired their impact and meaning from a conscious use of style and symbol. White Towers have a strict reason for being—hamburgers—and they remain, in whatever form, at the service of those ubiquitous meat patties.

SELECTED
WHITE TOWERS
1926-1972

Milwaukee #1 (1926)

The first shop included most of the characteristic elements of all future White Towers: it was a simple white building of a shiny material with a tower over the entrance.

Milwaukee #5 (1927)

The stock double-hung windows illustrate the modest nature of the early White Towers. They also strike a curious residential note for an imageful commercial building.

Los Angeles #1 (1928)

Early White Tower interiors were clean but plain. Food and graphic displays had not begun to achieve their ornamental and advertising potential.

Milwaukee #10 (1928)
Just a few touches of corbeling and
colored brick managed to give the
building a "medieval" appearance.

Milwaukee #10 (1928)

In contrast to the exterior, Milwaukee #10 gave no hint of medieval feasting inside.

Truck, Milwaukee (1929)

In the early years, all aspects of White Tower operations contributed to the company image. This tower truck made deliveries to the Milwaukee shops. It was not a rolling hamburger stand.

Racine #2 (1929)

The symbolic impact of the building as a whole was strengthened by placing the hamburger sign on a white background and allowing it to merge with the building's surface.

Milwaukee #1 (1929)

When Milwaukee #1 was moved from its corner site to an unilluminated spot in the middle of the block, it was given lights and an elaborate sign to compensate for the reduced visibility.

Milwaukee #1 (1926)

Milwaukee #1 (1929)
The thinness of the tower weakened
the impression of medieval solidity.

Detroit #2 (1928)

White Tower made an effort to celebrate local and national holidays and events. On Thanksgiving Day in Detroit, everything was on the house.

Detroit #34 (1929)

"It was a matter of creating a
building that was sanitary, easy to
maintain and keep clean, with
speedy counter service. Actually to
feed the masses with a limited,
inexpensive menu."

Detroit #27 (1929)

"In Detroit, every White Tower was across the street or around the corner from an automobile factory."...

Detroit #40 (1929)

. . . or on a highly visible corner site
near mass transit.

Philadelphia #3 (1930)

"During the thirties, women didn't
work. They were home. It wasn't
the thing for a girl to work."

Rochester #1 (1931)

"There were very few plates used in a tower; nickel everything, pie and everything else. No ketchup, lots of mustard. We used to take a piece of paper out, put it on the counter, and put the hamburger on top. It was as simple as that. Then when we got real ritzy later on we went to plates."

**Delivery truck and
Milwaukee #1 (1929)**

The White Tower symbol had
shrunk to a tiny headdress, but the
truck was white and it did carry
the company's messages around
town. The building behind it is
Milwaukee #1 in its original corner
location.

**Delivery truck and
Detroit #13 (1929)**

This truck was a moving billboard
for the Detroit White Towers and
their local baker.

Minneapolis #2 (1929)

The small size of the White Towers
made them easy to move when
economic conditions demanded it.

Philadelphia #5 (1930)

Clarence Haffeman's assembly-line White Tower design of the early thirties substituted the more explicit imagery of rooftop crenelations for the simple style of the Milwaukee towers.

Boston #1 (1931)

The White Tower ideal was to be
"a well-illuminated individual
building having a corner location."

Tower # 1
283 Tremont St.
Boston, Mass.

Boston #8 (1932)

Painting the stonework black helped this White Tower stand out from its surroundings at the expense of shrinking its apparent size.

The Palm Garden behind Boston #8

New York #6 (1932)

A busy location was worth developing wherever it was found.

New York #1 (1930)

"In those days, we opened everything twenty-four hours a day, seven days a week. We'd open up and throw the key away. Once, Arnold called me and said, 'Why don't you come on home?' I couldn't. 'Why?' he asked. Nobody was working in Number One. He said, 'Close it.' With what? It didn't even have a door, only a screen door. You couldn't leave a place like that."

49

Boston #5 (1932)

Corners were always an opportunity. Tight sites were never a deterrent.

New York #11 (1933)

Disengaging the edge of the tower from the building behind enhanced the effect of a freestanding White Tower.

New York #7 (1932)

The auxiliary sidewalk counter
attests to the value of this location
under the stair to the Brooklyn
Bridge. It is clear that White Tower
would accept any distortion of its
building in order to operate in such
a profitable place.

New York #7 (1932)
The columns that supported the
stairway pierced this White Tower
and defined its limits.

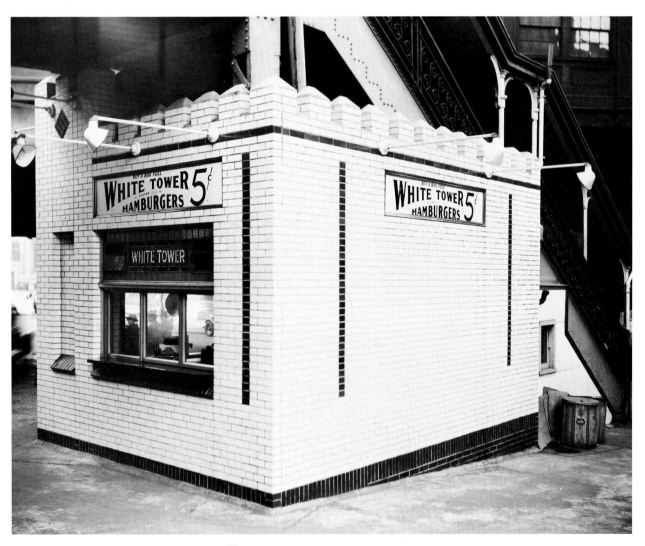

Philadelphia #8 (1932)

"When I first came with the
company, the towers were basically
smaller. Actually, if they had ten
seats, it was a pretty good-sized
tower."

Philadelphia #8 (1932)

"And then we started putting booths in the towers for the ladies to come in and sit down."

Philadelphia #9 (1932)

By 1932, more than half of the
stations along the Broad Street
subway had White Towers near
the top of their steps.

Philadelphia #9 (1932)

"At first, when the White Tower started, a lot of people were afraid of the hamburgers. That's why I prepared them in the window, so that people could actually see the product that they were getting. We're very quality conscious."

Pittsburgh #11 (1931)
The local codes demanded no less
than a two-story building on this
site.

Pittsburgh #14 (1932)

"We now have booths and are ready
for beer to come back," say both
the note on the back of this
photograph and the absence of
stools at the counter.

Minneapolis #1 (1929)

This early attempt to change the imagery of the White Tower was ultimately unsuccessful since it failed to replace the medieval trappings with a version of the modern style that was equally arresting.

Chicago #1 (1928)

This was White Tower's most radical experiment with the Moderne. The Vitrolite tower was skillfully abstracted into a stepped motif, and the sign was elevated and illuminated as a separate extravaganza, but the effect was far too stylish. It did not reinforce the chain image, so the approach was dropped.

New York #10 (1933)

The Vitrolite Company built New
York #10 for White Tower to show
what its product could do. Its
extravagant use of materials made
it too expensive to be reproduced,
but its appearance became the
model for White Tower's shift to
a modern style.

New York #10 (1933)

"In the daytime it was beautiful,
and at night it was better."

New York #10 (1933)

"CLEAN as a whistle. Just look at
this White Tower. Notice how
CLEANLINESS predominates. This
is your assurance of being served
with pure and wholesome food."

Syracuse #1 (1934)

"In those days the more 'gingerbread' there was, the more luxurious it was."

Syracuse #1 (1934)

Syracuse #1 (1934)

Once a technique for joining and
waterproofing porcelain enamel was
developed, both the exterior and
the interior could be clad in the
same material.

Syracuse #1 (1934)

Now, on entering the shop, the customer's visual expectations were literally fulfilled.

New York #13 (1934)

"Turnover in help, we didn't have too much. In the shops, a guy had to be around six or seven years, ten years, before he'd get to be a manager, let alone a supervisor. Back in those days, they didn't have hardly any turnover. You worked a twelve- or fourteen-hour day, seven days a week, and it didn't bother you. Everyone enjoyed it."

New York #13 (1934)

"A guy would have to roll a couple
hundred pounds of hamburger
before he quit. We opened up with
three hundred pounds a day. All
hand rolled, all by hand."

Philadelphia #11 (1935)

By eliminating the colored pilasters and floral appliqué on the tower, the overall impact of the building was strengthened.

Philadelphia #11 (1935)

"It used to be the rule the night crew took care of the inside of the building and the day crew took care of the outside of the building, in between customers."

71

Scranton #1 (1936)

"The tower could be slightly dirty on the inside or outside, but if the windows were clean it always looked good."

Scranton #1 (1936)

"Guys like Bernie Gooch used to put toothpicks in the corner of the refrigerator to see whether you'd cleaned it or not. It didn't make a difference how clean it was. If the toothpick was there you hadn't cleaned it."

Hartford #1 (1935)

"A building like this could be under construction and there might be a sign on it saying 'corner for lease.' J. E. would be there to pick up the corner."

Lynn (Mass.) #1 (1935)

"You put up a breakfast sign, a luncheon sign, and the afternoon sign was 'Be Sure It's A White Tower.' And God help you if you came in at noontime and had that breakfast sign up."

Springfield (Mass.) #1 (1935)

"I think the idea to keep it limited
was to produce a few things well."

New York #5 (1935)

"Actually the first year I was with White Tower I did about thirty locations, but they were not as sophisticated as what we have to do today."

Boston #12 (1936)

"In January 1936, I had to go up to Boston. We had a small front, about nine feet, so working that small front in, that's the first time I came up with this screwy tower which I never really liked."

Window displays

"If you don't have variety for them
they're going to go down the street.
You must have variety. They're not
going to eat a hamburger five days
a week."

79

Paterson #1 (1935)

Architect B. Sumner Gruzen solved
the problems of a difficult site to
produce a large, streamlined tower
that was to be a source of stylistic
inspiration for later designs.

Paterson #1 (1935)

"Gruzen was a designer, and I liked his exterior a lot better than the interior because he used an awful lot of curvatures, and curvatures ran into extra money. Curved glass got to be a headache."

Plan of Paterson #1 (1935)

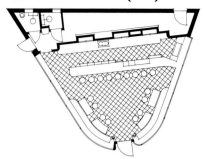

Paterson #1 (1935)

The effects of horizontality and continuity in the facade were consciously expressed in the treatment of the message panel and counter inside.

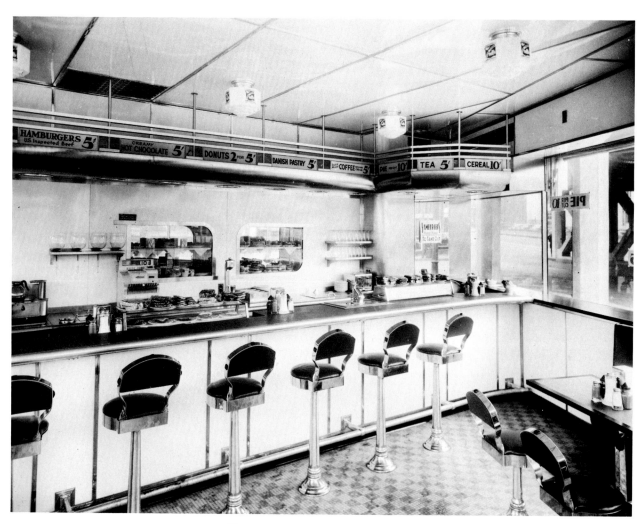

Camden #5 (1936)

Camden #5 was bought by White Tower in 1941. It had been built in 1936 by local entrepreneurs. The building was already a porcelain enamel box with a central tower and gooseneck lamps, all basic White Tower elements.

Camden #5 (1936)

The interior was clad in tile rather than porcelain enamel, but the effect was the same as with all other White Towers.

Camden #5 (1936)

The large sweep of glass ended with
a curve in the manner of the
Cushman Bakeries in New York.

Baltimore #1 (1936)

The awnings might strike an incongruous note on a self-consciously "modern" White Tower, but they were necessary in pre–air conditioning days for a building with such large windows.

Baltimore #1 (1936)

"This is where I first put the griddle out so a customer could be greeted properly. When he came in he was greeted with 'hello.' When he left it was 'good-bye.'"

New York #18 (1936)

During the mid-thirties, the Saxes were attracted to the possibilities of placing White Towers on suburban sites along major roadways so they could serve customers who traveled in automobiles as well as on trolleys and subways.

New York #18 (1936)

"New York #18 was one of my
first attempts at making them a
little larger. That building was
thirty-two feet by eighteen feet.
I had ten stools at the counter and
ten at the window shelf."

Baltimore #2 (1936)

"All day long you waited on
business people, the cab drivers, and
at night you had the chorus girls.
You had everybody going there."

Rochester #5 (1937)

"J. E. would watch a location for years and years. He would delve in to get the facts of a location. Some of these places he was even watching for as long as ten years. Because there was a house on it, that didn't worry him. If he was interested in it, he would watch it, and then pick it up."

Baltimore #3 (1936)

"You had to wash the windows. Had those little stickers. The windows would steam up and the signs would fall and you'd run like hell to put them back up again before the supervisor came around."

Troy #1 (1936)

"Think of all I did in 1936. You didn't have time to sit down and restudy. You had to get moving."

Philadelphia #1 (1939)

"I visualized what they were doing from the brick building that they had, so I tried to get something like it in a similar format but covering it under porcelain. They had covered a few stores in porcelain, but I did not think they had the zip that this thing did."

Philadelphia #1 (1930)

94

Boston #1 (1938)

"Then after a while we were somewhat criticized for our tower. So Mr. J. E. asked me, 'Now, what's the reason for the tower?' He said the tower wasn't functional. I said, 'I'll tell you how we can make the tower functional. We'll put a clock up there.' "

Boston #1 (1931)

95

Boston #5 (1938)

"I think the best thing that ever happened was when we covered them. Then they looked clean, once you cleaned them."

Boston #5 (1932)

Philadelphia #8 (1939)

This renovation was an opportunity to change the original proportions of the tower to increase its impact.

Philadelphia #8 (1932)

Philadelphia #2 (1937)

Only seven years after it was built, Philadelphia #2 was covered in porcelain enamel sheets both outside . . .

Philadelphia #2 (1930)

Philadelphia #2 (1937)

. . . and inside.

Food display

"The big deal was mass displays. If you had only one piece of pie up, you'd never sell it."

Food display

"Put up ten or twelve pies, and
you'll sell it."

New York #17 (1936)

"Actually I never thought that the
tower design was any good, but all
I tried to do was create a tower
formation with some ornamentation
on it so it would look a little rich."

Washington #3 (1936)

"This building is in the middle of the block, but our property went back about a hundred feet. Mr. Saxe said, 'Come in here and create an alley so it looks like an individual building.' Our locations were often in the interior of a block. If there was an alley there we would consider it as good a thing as a corner location."

New York #16 (1936)

Here, because of site and structural conditions, the entrance could not take its normal position under the tower, which remained on the corner of the building for greater visibility. As a result, this shop looks as if it is being pulled in two directions.

Providence #4 (1937)

This tower, although tied to the door, was hopelessly constrained by the circumstances of the site, but it had to appear in some form. "Tower" was, after all, the company symbol and part of the company name.

Providence #3 (1937)

A steel frame allowed the glass to wrap completely around the front of this shop.

Detroit #46 (1940)

With the addition of a porcelain enamel skin, Detroit #46 looked just like the newest shops. Only the relatively small window and the bits of wall surface around it hint of a masonry structure behind.

Detroit #46 (1929)

Menands (N.Y.) #1 (1936)

"The owner of White Tower insisted on a rounded corner. . . . He asked, 'Will the rounded corners be expensive?' I said yes, and he asked, 'Will they be so expensive that other people may not be able to afford them?' When I said, 'It might be,' he said, 'Then I want them.' "

Camden #2 (1937)

"Let's try a center tower, because
with a center tower you don't need
a right or a left."

Camden #4 (1938)

"We had this big lot and this little building."

Philadelphia #12 (1937)

"J. E. always wanted the building
right out to the property line and as
long as he wanted it that's where
I put it."

Philadelphia #12, opening night

Boston #13 (1937)

"Many towers turned out to be a piece of advertising just by themselves. In other words, put a little more money in the building so you could spend less money in advertising."

New York #24 (1938)

"Of course then we did junk it up with a lot of signs, but it wasn't so much the aesthetics of it. It was a matter of getting the people in to eat. We're in business to make a buck."

New York #24 (1938)

New York #19 (1936)

"We worked that to death, that
side window. Fifty-six nickel
hamburgers on that griddle every
three minutes."

New York #19 (1936)

"We always worked on the premise of a lot of glass. In our smaller buildings I think proportionately we used as much glass if not more than any of the others. We have always been very glass conscious."

New York #10A (1938)

"We were located on bus lines,
trolley lines, and subway lines."

Buffalo #IA (1938)

The enlarged tower of Buffalo #IA sits comfortably on the building below, and its decoration clarifies its connection to the entrance. It is a significant improvement over previous roadside shops whose small towers were not scaled to the building or the open sites on which they were placed.

Washington #4 (1938)

The roadside central tower design was adapted to downtown sites, although circumstances in town usually favored a tower and an entrance on a corner.

Washington #5 (1938)

The freestanding White Tower effect could be achieved by manipulating the building's skin, projecting bays slightly forward of the tower and covering the parapet in contrasting black porcelain enamel.

Washington #5 (1938)

"In Washington, D.C., I would go into the building with the plan examiners, and by the time I got finished with them they would say to me, 'This isn't a building, it's a machine.'"

Buffalo #5 (1938)

"Orange juice came in about 1938. There was a cafeteria on 57th Street and this fellow, boy, he was really squeezing out the oranges. So J. E. brought me around and said, 'Look what he's doing.' Fresh orange juice where the customer could see it squeezed. That was the deal because a lot of restaurants did squeeze in the back room and then put water in it."

Truck, Pittsburgh (1937)

"Well, you see, we never stayed stagnant but would make improvements that the average layman would not see or sense, but we knew the improvements we were making. It was like an automobile."

Truck, Milwaukee (1929)

Camden #3 (1938)

The first deluxe White Tower—twice as big as the normal shops with three times as many seats—was built directly across the road from Camden #2. It was called "Marbett's" (a combination of the names of T. E. Saxe's sisters, Margaret and Betty) to maintain the appearance of direct competition.

Camden #3 (1938)

"When we first built this, J. E.,
boy, he was standing across the
street mumbling. He thought it was
terrific."

Camden #3 (1938)

"We did well at Number Three because there was nothing else around. People would drive a mile or so just to get to our place. They got to like it."

Camden #3 (1938)

"That was Chuck Clements in the middle there, the curb fellow that we had in charge of the girls."

Carhops at Camden #3 (1938)
"The girls used to work the curb
from 11:00 in the morning until
2:00 AM, 3:00 AM on weekends."

Silver Spring #1 (1938)

The implied motion of Silver
Spring's streamlining makes it
appear the speediest machine in the
parking lot.

Silver Spring #1 (1938)

The carhops had their own entrance
and exit in the projecting wing on
the parking lot side. Once inside
they shared the back counter and
griddle with the countermen.

Silver Spring #1 (1938)

This dining room reached the apex
of White Tower elegance in cool
porcelain enamel, bright stainless
steel, and jazzy tile.

Silver Spring #1 (1938)

"The reason we had tile floors and porcelain walls and ceilings was because these poor people had to Bon Ami the floor, walls, and ceiling once a week. With all this metal they had to glisten."

Silver Spring #1 (1938)
Instead of the standard gooseneck lamps, the projecting canopy supported the lighting fixtures and emphasized the streamlining with its neon trim. For a deluxe building it was appropriate that its most important sign, floating in space at night above the tower, said "Restaurant" rather than "White Tower."

Silver Spring #1 (1938)

"It was a restaurant. It had sodas, full-course meals, and sundaes, and we sold beer on the curb there. But I tore out the beer line. Had to. Nobody could serve beer. You had to be twenty-one to serve beer and there was no one on the payroll who was twenty-one."

Richmond #1 (1939)

"I always worked on the premise, hoping that what I did would be good today and good twenty or twenty-five years from now."

Richmond #1 (1939)
The paper icicles on the window
called attention to the new air
conditioning inside.

Washington #2A (1940)

White Tower also built the stores to the left, carefully keeping them black to make the White Tower stand out. "Between the stores, the White Tower, and the parking in the back, we made money on it. That was J. E.'s theory of real estate. In other words, try to pick something so you make money on it and you get free rent."

Washington #2A (1940)

Washington #2A (1940)

Here, for the first time, the tower was used purely as a signpost. Charles Johnson designed the large, stylish, three-dimensional letters with black edging to give them an illuminated quality.

Washington #2A (1940)

Paterson #1 (1945)

"During the war . . . the wives went
out and worked to subsidize the
husband's salary."

Towerettes (1939, 1942, 1946, 1947)
"Things really changed after World
War II."

1939

1942

1946

1947

Dayton #3 (1941)

"Sure, these buildings are nice and
white and shiny and pure. They did
look rich, and people would ask,
'How can they afford to sell a nickel
hamburger?' The answer to that is
that we built them well to eliminate
maintenance."

Baltimore #6 (1941)

"During the war we weren't building. It was up to me to keep these places in business, and by going around it gave me a chance to see what I thought were some of the defects. Some of the places I thought could be improved upon as far as sanitation was concerned."

Rochester #2 and #2A (1941)

"We lost our lease because a large parking lot was going in, so we built an adjacent building. It's a peculiar thing. For one week these two establishments were open at the same time."

Rochester #2 (1932)

Rochester #2A (1941)

Philadelphia #13 (1941)

From an advertising point of view,
this tower took a backward step,
since it had removed its symbolic
"medieval" and "Moderne"
decorative motifs, but had not yet
replaced them with signs.

143

Boston #14 (1940)

During the day, the White Tower, the flower shop, and the movie theater had a similar impact on the street . . .

Boston #1 (1940)

Boston #14 (1940)

. . . but at night, the overall lighting
on the porcelain enamel made
Boston #14 the most visible shop
on the block by far. It even upstaged
the movie theater, a traditional
nighttime extravaganza.

Baltimore #8 (1948)

"An advertising man took my letters
and devised the slash *T*. All of a
sudden he came in with it and I
said to myself, 'Why didn't I think
of that?' "

Baltimore #8 (1948)

"The whole point of the tower was
to reflect light off its shell."

Rochester #2A (1941)

"With a White Tower we never played shades and shadows; it was more or less a good, clean, white building."

**Hollywood mock-up (1948) for
"The Babe Ruth Story," starring
William Bendix as Babe Ruth**

"We've never really made a
determination, but I'll dare say 90
percent of it is nothing but local
business. It's not transit. They know
us."

Detroit #34A (1946)

"This was the first time after the war that I really saw the severe increase of building costs, of about 25 percent. That really had me concerned. I was aggravated about it, but there was nothing you could do."

Philadelphia #8A (1946)

White Tower lost its corner lease, so it built this new shop in a storefront next door. The tower with its cantilevered sign continued to grow in importance, but not as much as the enlarged windows emphasizing the view inside.

Philadelphia #8 (1932)

Philadelphia #8 (1939)

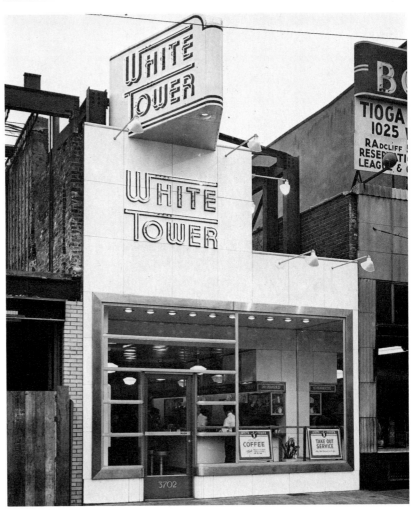

Philadelphia #14 (1947)

"So I've always worked on the philosophy that competition brings business, providing you're the best."

Philadelphia #14 (1947)

Springfield (Mass.) #1 (1947)
The White Tower was scaled up and simplified. So was the optometrist's office next door.

Springfield (Mass.) #1 (1935)

Milwaukee #12 (1949)

The corner column was mirrored,
so that the effect of wrap-around
glass was not diminished, although
the trick was unmasked at night.

Milwaukee #12 (1949)

Buffalo #4 (1956)

In this renovation, the area of white
porcelain above the window was
reduced to give more prominence
to the tower.

Buffalo #4 (1938)

Stamford #1 (1949)

A large expanse of fixed plate glass could emphasize the building's giant scale. Although the windows covered more than half the building's surface, the glass did not detract from the impact of the cubic form or the effect of whiteness, since the interiors were white as well.

Moving New York #6A (1949)

Moving New York #6 was a two-day process. Since the building could travel only at night it had to spend one day on the road sitting below the Hall of Fame at New York University.

Stamford #2 (1951)

In the 1950s, White Tower bought fifteen prefabricated buildings from the Valentine Manufacturing Company. Johnson then modified the basic Valentine steel frame, only ten feet by twenty-five feet, which was used for house and motel units, as well as hamburger stands.

Stamford #2 (1951)

"Well, in their brochure they had
little puny windows, little doors.
I went in there and I said, 'Do it
this way.' When we got on the job
we put up porcelain enamel on it,
then we put up the facing, four sides
of the tower."

Stamford #2 (1951)

"When we first bought them, I told management it was a ten year proposition. At the end of ten years, we'll just have to dump it and put another one on in its place. Of course, we never did that."

Richmond #5 (1950)

"So I got a good shot of 'White Tower' here and then the word 'Hamburgers' here."

Stamford #2 (1951)

"I think that we've gone about as far as we can go in the White Towers. I really don't feel that with the size of our units that we can add. We just can't. We're tight. We're tight as we are and I just don't. . . ."

Portsmouth (Va.) #1 (1951)

"Management seemed to like them,
and our city managers liked them.
It was something that they could
handle easily."

Richmond #5 (1950)

The building was a sign, but a large
roadside sign was used as well. This
large, freestanding sign, with 'Coca-
Cola' symbolically dominating
'White Tower,' was evidence of a
new order along the highway and
also of White Tower's dwinding
confidence in the ability of its
building to carry the entire symbolic
burden by itself.

164

Philadelphia #17 (1954)

"For a sign on a building, the sign enhances the design and it's a peculiar thing. Normally a sign detracts."

New Rochelle #2 (1954)

With the stylishly outlined "White Tower" placed redundantly on the actual white tower, the tower became both a symbol and a signpost.

New Rochelle #2 (1954)

"From the very beginning we cooked to order. We never cooked ahead; we still do not cook ahead. Everything in White Tower is cooked to order to your desire."

Syracuse #4 (1953)

"Management does not know what
it's getting until it's built at times.
If they don't like it, it's a mistake.
If they don't make an indication,
they like it."

Atlantic City #2 (1955)

"We usually like to get a place right on the corner, so when we would take a place inside, I had to work out something so the people could see it."

Atlantic City #2 (1955)

Norfolk #3A (1956)

"If I didn't have it illuminated properly, the owners would say, 'Gee, it doesn't look right.' In other words, we didn't want any shadows around."

Detroit #40A (1954)

"It was the same on the interiors;
I had to get the interiors brightly
lit."

Camden #8 (1955)

"We get a lot of repeat business."

Philadelphia #17 (1954)

Camden #8 (1955)

Milwaukee #1 (1957)

"As a real estate man Mr. Saxe was very farsighted. He had a terrific knowledge of real estate. His main thing for a long period of time was it should be a white building. A white tower."

Milwaukee #1 (1926)

Milwaukee #1 (1929)

Riverdale #1 (1953)

"We still like the word 'hamburgers.'
Hamburgers, we think, bring in the
business."

New York #12 (1956)

This White Tower runs through a
building and out the other side,
reversing its facade in mirror image
when it gets there.

New York #12 (1934)

Philadelphia #5 (1952)

A pure cube style, the ultimate in
porcelain enamel technology, was
the ultimate solution for chain
consistency since it made renovations
indistinguishable from new
buildings. There is no way of
knowing that this White Tower was
twenty-two years old when it was
reclad, or that it is forty-eight years
old today.

Philadelphia #5 (1930)

Detroit #44 (1956)

"Our boys wanted expansion, wanted dinner items, but you have to remember that some of our units are thirty, forty years old. We just don't have the equipment or the space to put in all the convenience foods that you would like to put in. We tried to use the foods that we already had in the unit and make combinations that would make dinner items."

Detroit #44 (1929)

New York #13 (1954)

As the decorative elements, metal strips and contrasting base panels, were removed, New York #13 grew bolder in scale. The "modern" cantilevered corner is expressed in the last remodeling. The corner of the building had always been cantilevered, of course.

New York #13 (1934)

New York #13 (1936)

New York #16 (1956)

This remodeling changed the tower's emphasis from symbol to billboard but retained the original approach to the difficult site conditions, so the resolution of the tower with the entrance remains awkward.

New York #16 (1936)

Camden #2 (1957)

Making the tower a billboard was a logical evolution for roadside White Towers, which faced widened roadways filled with speeding automobiles.

Camden #2 (1937)

New York #23 (1957)

"In the outlying stores we did try to get family trade. At places like #23 we had coloring books to attract the kids to come in with their parents. If they colored the book, they'd get a free hamburger. We tried all sorts of stuff like that, but I don't think we were very successful with it."

New York #23 (1937)

Boston #13 (1960)

"Somehow or other, I don't know whether it's best to have a location going into a city or out of a city. I don't know whether it's best to have a location the far side of a stoplight or the short side. I really don't know as yet with all the places we have."

Boston #13 (1937)

Menands (N. Y.) #1 (1958)

As long as a White Tower remains in a busy location, it continues to prosper. The women standing in front, now twenty-two years older, are still waiting for their bus.

Menands (N. Y.) #1 (1936)

Pittsburgh #16A (1965)

"Because we had the color on there, it changed the entire image. It was almost like a complete alteration to the exterior. It changed the exterior feeling of the building."

Pittsburgh #16 (1946)

184

Norfolk #3B (1965)

This building was moved, enlarged, and given a carhop shed in the rear. Its sign was scaled up for the highway and its tower, shifted from the right end to the new center, was redecorated.

Norfolk #3A (1956)

185

Richmond #1 (1960)

"Well, you have to update. In
other words, you try to eliminate
obsolescence."

Richmond #1 (1939)

Raleigh #2 (1972)

"You also have to have a broader appeal, and the nickel hamburger image has to be eradicated by staying with modern taste yet with excellence of food."

Philadelphia #12 (1938)

"This building, the way it is here,
although it was built in 1938, is still
good today."

Camden #4 (1965)

"So if you were going to rank the order of importance, I guess having the right location—you've got to have that. Second, the internal layout. Third is the service, and fourth, maybe just the visual impact of the restaurant from the outside."

Geographical Index of White Towers